THE CHARLATANS MELTING POT

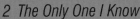

IMP

INTERNATIONAL MUSIC PUBLICATIONS LIMITED

ENGLAND: SOUTHEND ROAD,
WOODFORD GREEN, ESSEX IG8 8HN
GERMANY: MARSTALLSTR. 8. D-80539 MUNCHEN
DENMARK: DANMUSIK, VOGNMAGERGADE 7
DK 1120 KOBENHAVNK

WARNER/CHAPPELL MUSIC

CANADA: 85 SCARSDALE ROAD, SUITE 101
DON MILLS, ONTARIO, M3B 2R2
SCANDINAVIA: P.O. BOX 533, VENDEVAGEN 85 B
S-182 15, DANDERYD, SWEDEN
AUSTRALIA: P.O. BOX 353
3 TALAVERA ROAD, NORTH RYDE N.S.W. 2113

Nuova CARISH S.p.A.

ITALY: VIA CAMPANIA, 12
20098 S. GIULIANO MILANESE (MI)
ZONA INDUSTRIALE SESTO ULTERIANO
FRANCE: 25 RUE D'HAUTEVILLE,
75010 PARIS

WARNER BROS. PUBLICATIONS
THE GLOBAL LEADER IN PRINT

USA: 15800 NW 48TH AVENUE
MIAMI, FL 33014

Music Transcribed by Barnes Music Engraving Ltd., East Sussex TN22 4HA
Printed by The Panda Group · Haverhill · Suffolk CB9 8PR · UK · Binding by Oak Manor · Ipswich

The Only One I Know

Words and Music by Martin Blunt,
Robert Collins, Timothy Burgess,
Jon Baker and Jon Brookes

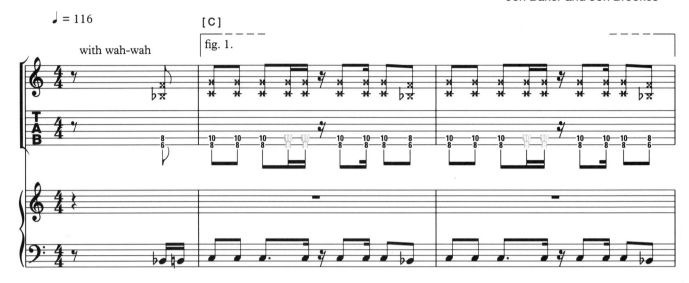

cont. sim.

C7   Bb

1. The on - ly___ one I know_____ storms will
2. The on - ly___ one I see_____ has found an

Eb   F   C7   Bb

take me a - way._____ The on - ly___ one I know_____ is mine when
ach-ing in me._____ The on - ly___ one I see_____ is stand - ing

Eb   F   C7

she stitch-es me.__
talk - ing to me.__

12.99

Ev-ery war_____ has been____

done be-fore_____ and ev-ery-bo - dy__ knows the pain.

The on - ly__ one I know_____ ne-ver cries ne - ver o - pens your eyes._____
The on - ly__ one I see_____ is mine__ when she walks down the street._____

Then

Words and Music by Martin Blunt,
Robert Collins, Timothy Burgess,
and Jon Brookes

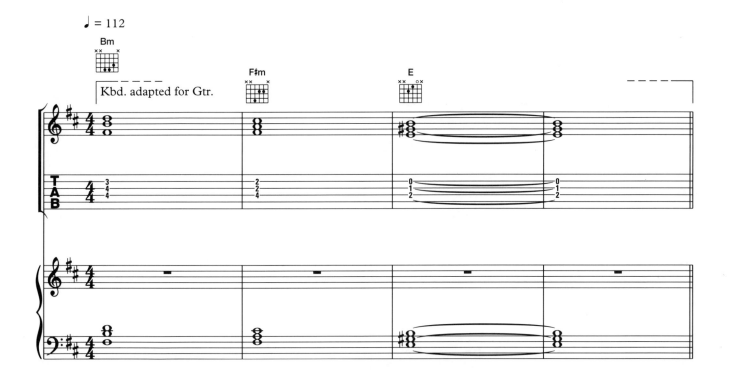

8

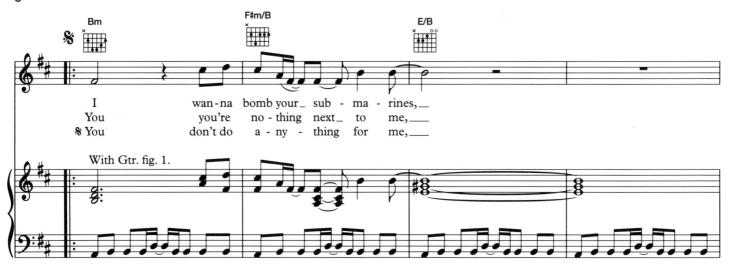

I wan-na bomb your sub-ma-rines,
You you're no-thing next to me,
You don't do a-ny-thing for me,

you don't do a-ny-thing for me.
I'm a phe-no-me-na you see.
we're a phe-no-me-na you see.

[E]

You were some-times hard to find, you were ne-ver safe to be with

10

Opportunity Three

Words and Music by Martin Blunt,
Timothy Burgess and Jon Brookes

[Bb]
Guitar tacet

A

1:33
1:52

Bb

(Keyboard chords)

boy with a strong - er e - mo - tion,   there's no-thing on me,___ I've got this
Loves ea - sy touch_ is per - fec - tion,   a   ba-lance of truth_ and cor - rec-

Over Rising

Words and Music by Martin Blunt,
Robert Collins, Timothy Burgess,
Jon Baker and Jon Brookes

Ov - er___ ris - ing,___ wash-ing me down_ a - gain,

2nd time   cont. sim.

with Gtr. fig. 2.

_____ ov - er___ ris - ing,___

wash-ing me down___ and now you're drown-ing me_ out._____ drown-ing me out.___

effects

Sproston Green
(US Version)

Words and Music by Martin Blunt,
Robert Collins, Timothy Burgess,
and Jon Baker

This one knows, she comes and goes,___

*4th time **to Coda** ⊕*

when she goes _____ she goes. _____

Spros-ton Green ___ she used to face ___ me _____
I know I'm too nec-es-sa - ry _____

and now she has - n't got ___ the time. _____
and ev - ery thing ___ she stole was mine. _____

(Keyboard chords)

Weirdo

Words and Music by Martin Blunt,
Robert Collins, Timothy Burgess,
and Jon Brookes

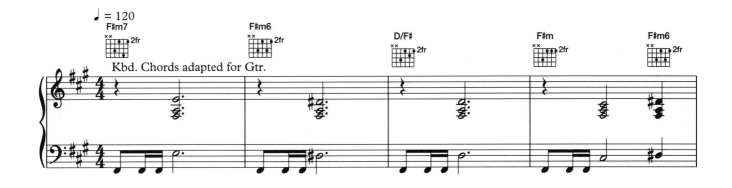

Most of the time you are hap-py,___ you're a weird-o,___
Most of the time you are hap-py,___ you're a wierd-o,___

and be-fore the in-tro-duc-tion, en-ter some-one feel-ing sor-ry for their___ selves.
and your nerve is my___ de-vice and it makes me___ sad.

Look at your___ ug-ly shame,___ what are you talk-ing___ for,

look at your____ ug - ly shame,_ there's too much for me to know a-bout.

there's too much   for me to know a-bout.

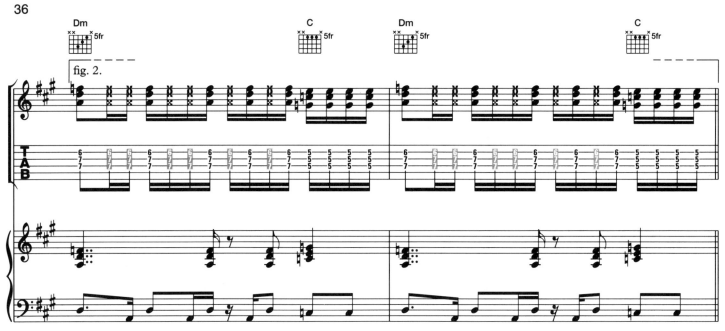

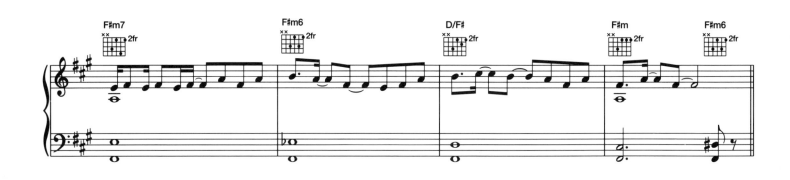

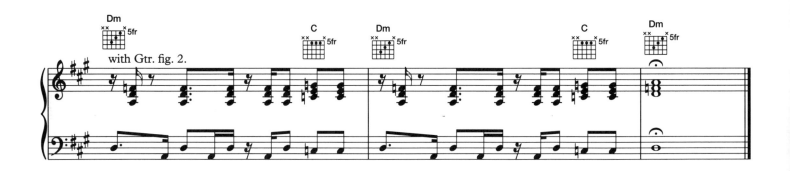

Theme From The Wish

By Martin Blunt, Robert Collins,
Mark Collins and Jon Brookes

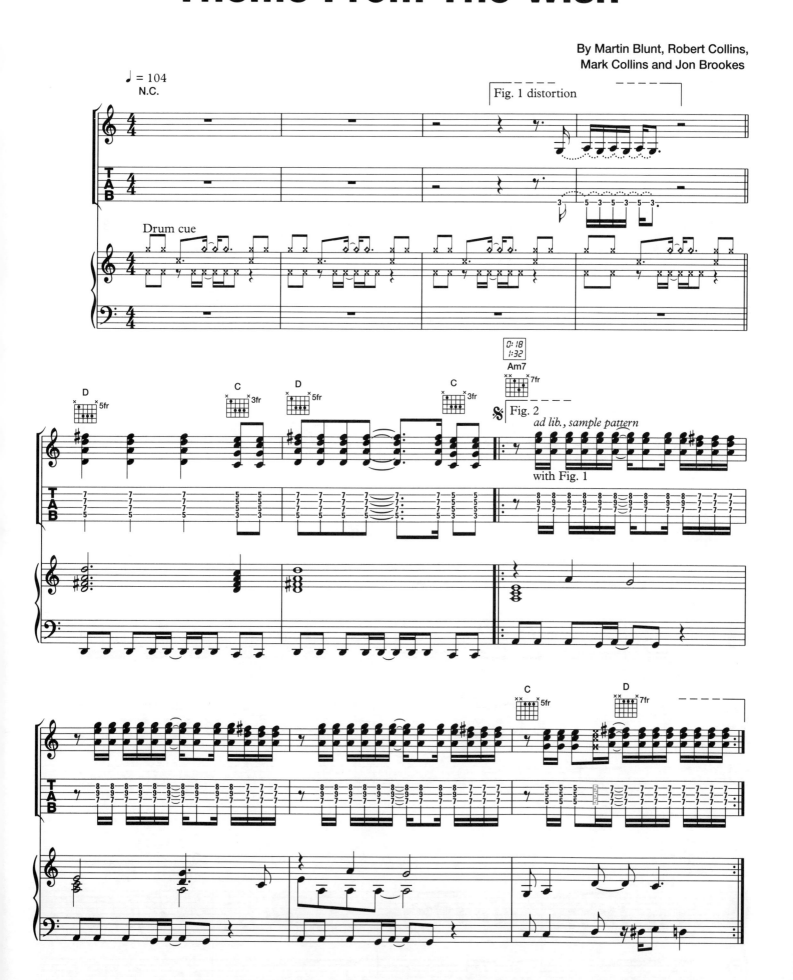

Patrol
(The Chemical Brothers Mix)

Words and Music by Martin Blunt,
Robert Collins, Timothy Burgess,
Mark Collins and Jon Brookes

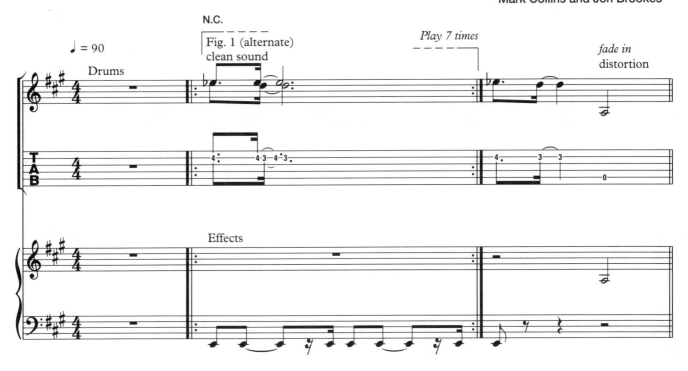

Play 7 times

Effects

with Figs. 1 & 2

2:01

Play 16 times

with Figs. 1 & 2

Less of the__ mad - ness, of the__ mad -

- ness, of the mad-ness,__ of the mad_____ mad.__

2:22

D

Less of the mad-ness, of the mad - ness, of the mad-ness, _ of the mad_____

_ mad._

Less of the mad-ness, of the mad - ness, of the mad-ness, _ of the mad_____

Sun comes up, ___ sun comes down ___ on a wave ___ to get the ～ ～ ～ ～ to

Can't Get Out Of Bed

Words and Music by Martin Blunt,
Robert Collins, Timothy Burgess,
Mark Collins and Jon Brookes

keep on, get it to - ge - ther.
go-ing off to no - where.

It's ev - ery-thing you
You're noth-ing that you

fig. 2.

want it to be_____ and want it to be_____ and want it to be._____
want-ed to be,_____ want-ed to be,_____ want-ed to be._____

1st time
only

Don't

Can't come in the road,_____ you fill in the holes_____ and ru - in your clothes.

Can't get out of bed_____ there's noth-ing and no-one's com-ing ov-er to me_____ there.

with Gtr. fig. 2.

There's noth-ing that you want-ed to be_____ or

I Never Want An Easy Life If Me And He Were Ever To Get There

Words and Music by Martin Blunt,
Robert Collins, Timothy Burgess
and Jon Brookes

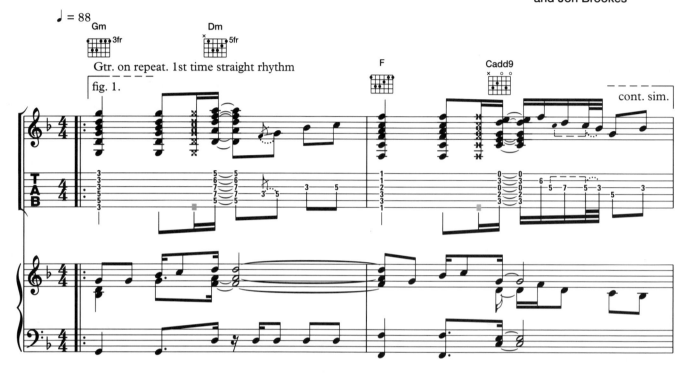

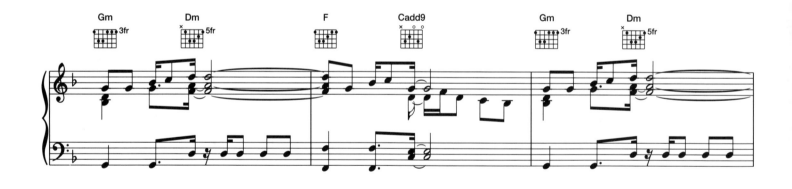

Save me, I wan-na stick with the signs, you shoot it up and go for a ride.
T. V. cul-ture is on-ly a start, you ov-er-pose, it's part of a gui-tar.

How is it I

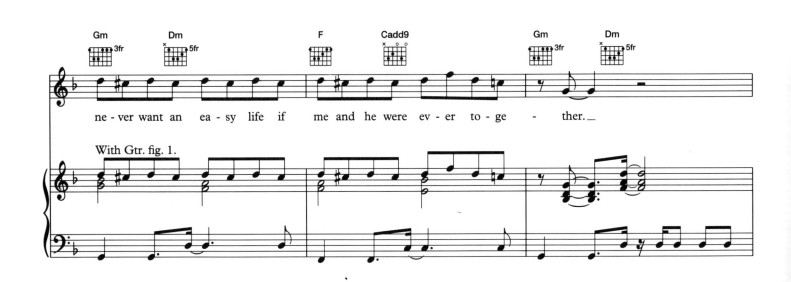

ne-ver want an ea-sy life if me and he were ev-er to-ge - ther.

With Gtr. fig. 1.

How is it I ne-ver want an ea-sy life if me and he were ev-er to-ge-

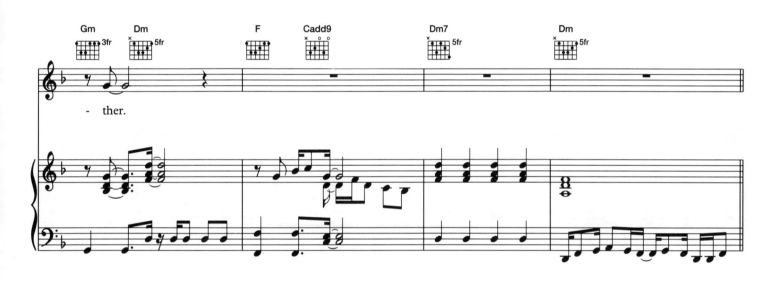

- ther.

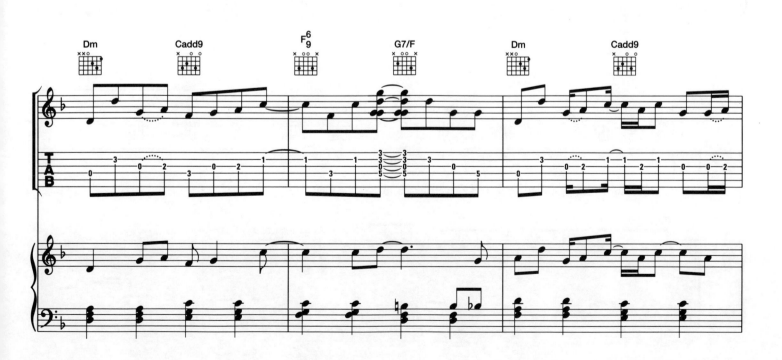

ne - ver want an ea-sy life if   me and he were ev-er to-ge   -   ther.

With Gtr. fig. 1.

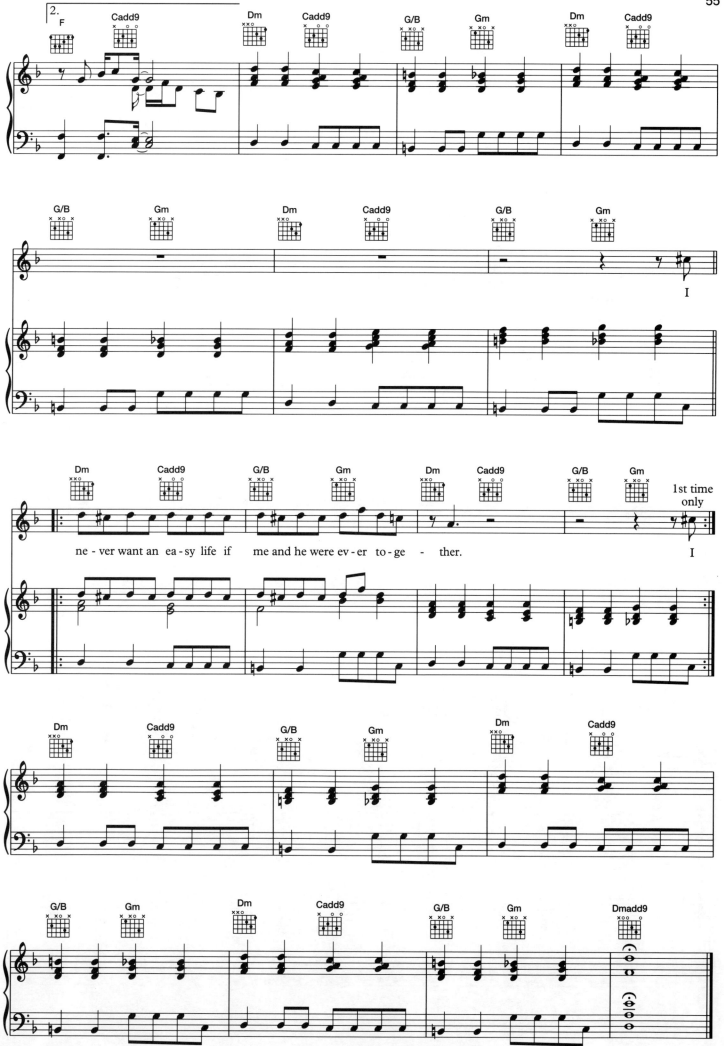

ne - ver want an ea - sy life if me and he were ev - er to - ge - ther.

Jesus Hairdo

Words and Music by Martin Blunt,
Robert Collins, Timothy Burgess,
Mark Collins and Jon Brookes

Boxes are Kbd. chords adapted for Gtr.

Gtr. 2.
Standard
tuning

Rhy. fig. 1.

Leave us____ I'm__ in hea-ven and I can't be-lieve I'm watch-ing you__ when
Fix our____ hands to - ge - ther when I surf, a-no-ther wave comes right, don't

ev-ery-thing you float up-on__ comes down too soon. Je-sus____ hair-do, I__ mean we
wan-na cry, know what I need, oh choose your words. Je-sus____ hair-do, I__ mean we

Sing your song when - ev - er, can't you see you're catch-ing some-thing I need. ___

cont. sim.

Get your-self to - ge-ther now, you're com-ing, com-ing out of the phase. ___

[B]

Crashin' In

Words and Music by Martin Blunt,
Robert Collins, Timothy Burgess,
Mark Collins and Jon Brookes

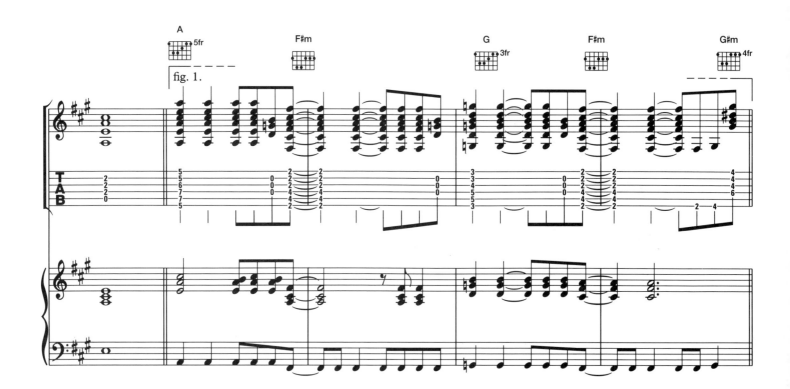

See me_ I can feel it com-ing a - round._

Yeah,_____ yeah.

repeat ad lib. to fade

Just Lookin'

Words and Music by Martin Blunt,
Robert Collins, Timothy Burgess,
Mark Collins and Jon Brookes

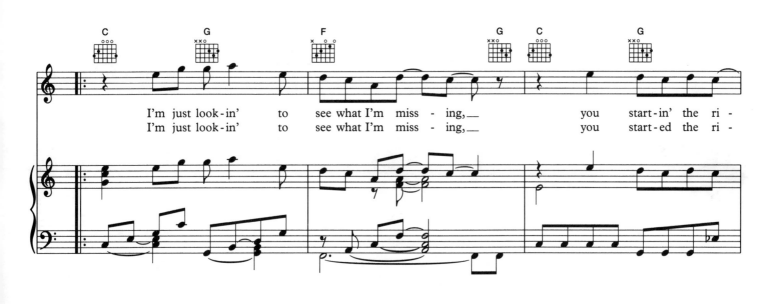

I'm just look-in' to see what I'm miss - ing,__ you start-in' the ri -
I'm just look-in' to see what I'm miss - ing,__ you start-ed the ri -

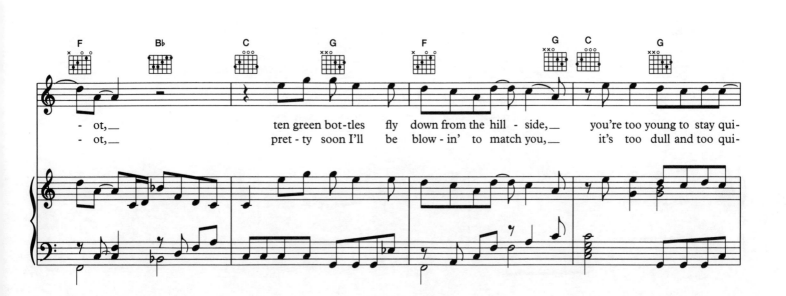

- ot,__ ten green bot-tles fly down from the hill - side,__ you're too young to stay qui-
- ot,__ pret-ty soon I'll be blow-in' to match you,__ it's too dull and too qui-

- et.___ Find a seat on your own___ train,_ I wan-na
- et,___ I bet you___ talk a-bout free - dom,_ and then

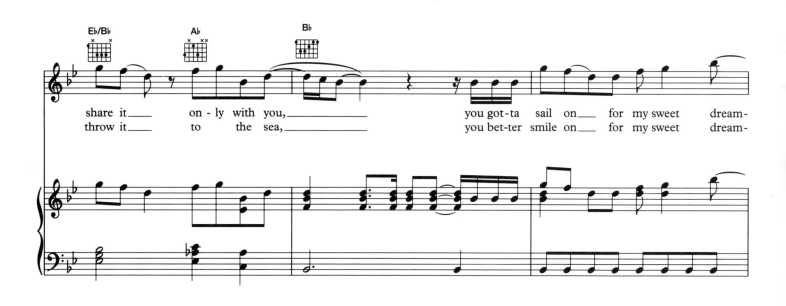

share it___ on - ly with you,_____ you got-ta sail on___ for my sweet dream-
throw it___ to the sea,_____ you bet-ter smile on___ for my sweet dream-

- er, I'll ne-ver take it a - way___ from you.___
- er, you'll ne-ver take it a - way___ from me.___

Yeah we stand with our hands in the air,_____ and we're feel - ing so good 'cause we care,

_____ and we're freak - ing a - bout_ in the bush,_____ feel - ing good feel-ing high_ it's a rush,

72

count me in 'cause I don't wan-na work, ___ in no place in the whole u-ni-verse. ___

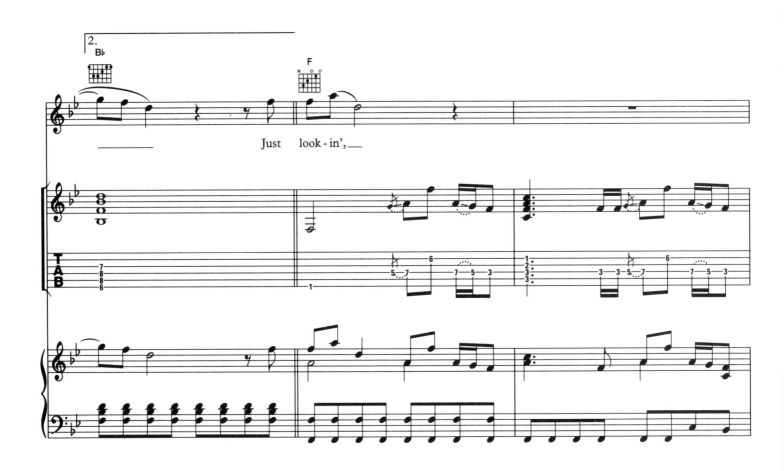

Just look-in', ___

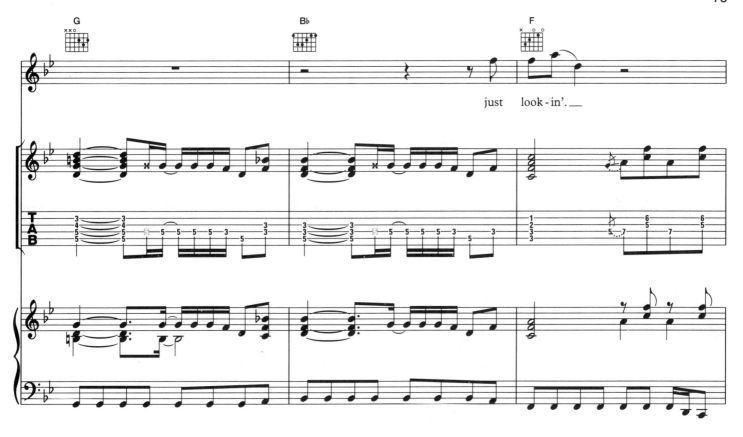

look - in', ___   just   look - in'. ___

Here Comes A Soul Saver

Words and Music by Martin Blunt,
Robert Collins, Timothy Burgess,
Mark Collins and Jon Brookes

Here comes a soul sa - ver_____ on your re-cord play - er, float - ing a-bout in the dust.

2. Tell me I'm sweet-er_____ than your bro-ken lead-er, I'll take the smooth with the rough.

drive____ in the sun-shine of ____ my life,   in the sun-shine of your life.____   Can you feel it when it's right?

Can you feel it in____ your soul?   Can you feel what's go-ing on?____   Yeah,   yeah

right.

with Fig. 2

Slide Gtr. ad lib.

Fig. 4
let ring

2:02

with Fig. 4

2:26

Don't kick it I want to freeze_ it, don't feel it I wan-na

Just When You're Thinkin' Things Over

Words and Music by Martin Blunt,
Robert Collins, Timothy Burgess,
Mark Collins and Jon Brookes

Just when you're think-ing things ov-er, and you need a set of vows,
I found you soak-ing in li-quid, I found you there in your
Just when you're think-ing things ov-er, oh yeah, you found your set of vows,

Right now___ where do you come from,___ kick up, go find your

sing a-ny - more, I'm com-ing home.

repeat ad lib. to fade

One To Another

Words and Music by Timothy Burgess,
Martin Blunt, Robert Collins,
Jon Brookes and Mark Collins

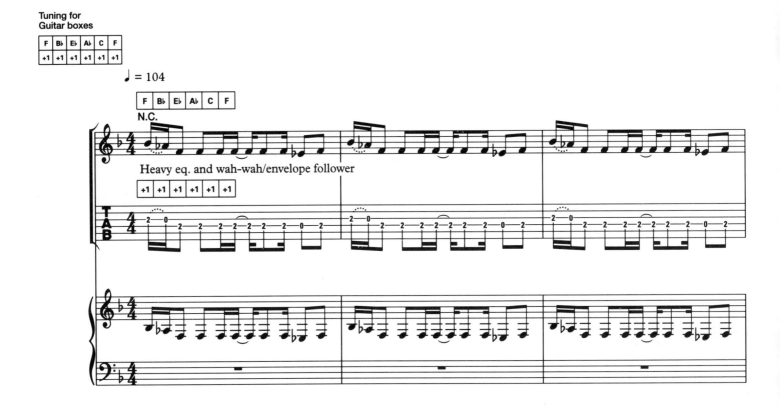

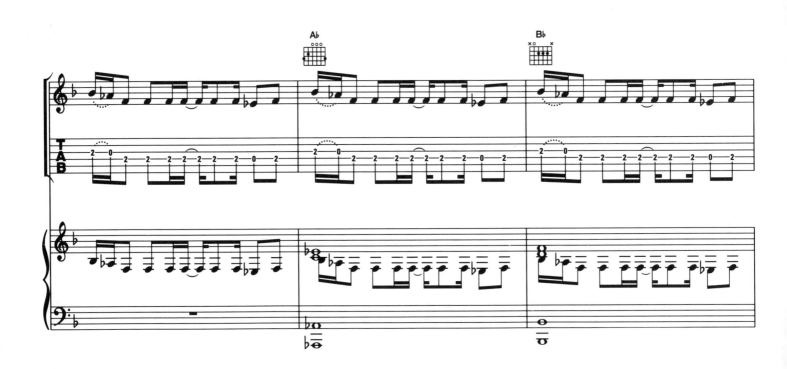

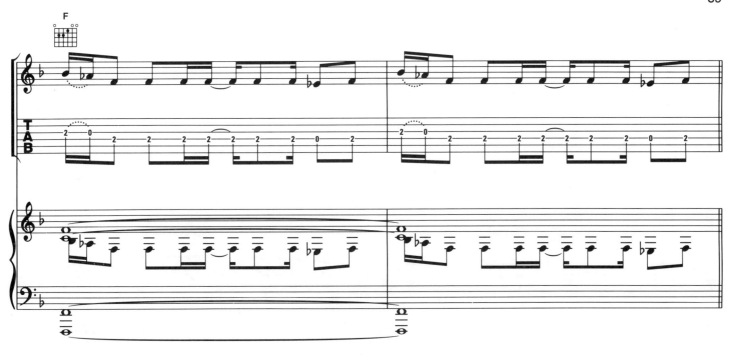

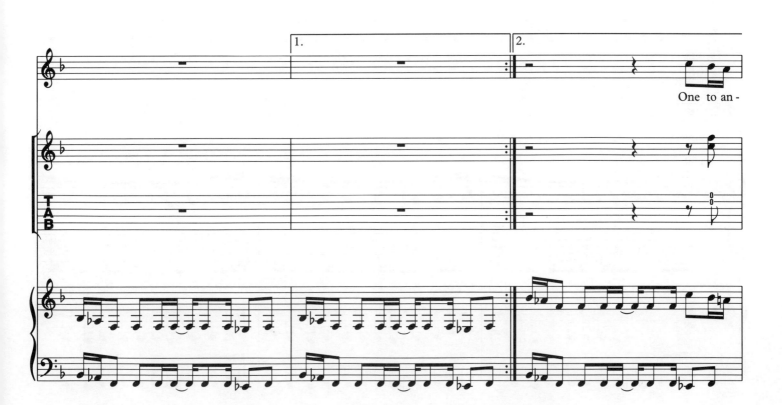

One to an -

Love, I a-dore you, al-ways look-ing for you, and I'll be ___

___ there when-ev-er you need ___ me. Be ___ my spi-der wo-man, I'll be ___

___ your spi-der-man.

Gtr. fig. 1

I

hurt you.

Stand

North Country Boy

Words and Music by Timothy Burgess,
Martin Blunt, Robert Collins,
Jon Brookes and Mark Collins

Hey   coun-try boy,_____   hey   coun-try boy._____   What are you

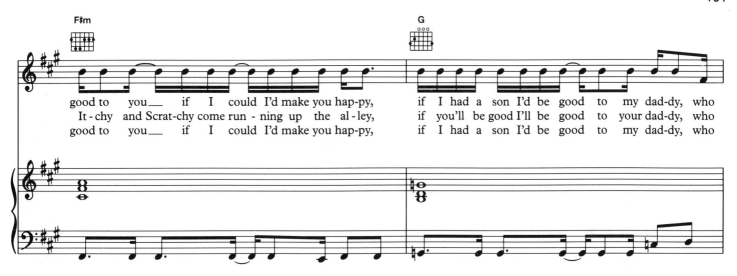

good to you__ if I could I'd make you hap-py, if I had a son I'd be good to my dad-dy, who
It-chy and Scrat-chy come run-ning up the al-ley, if you'll be good I'll be good to your dad-dy, who
good to you__ if I could I'd make you hap-py, if I had a son I'd be good to my dad-dy, who

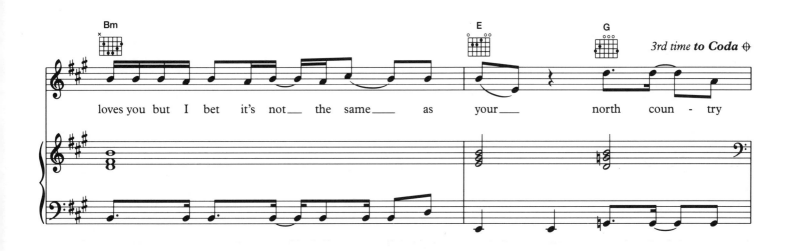

loves you but I bet it's not__ the same__ as your__ north coun-try

3rd time to Coda

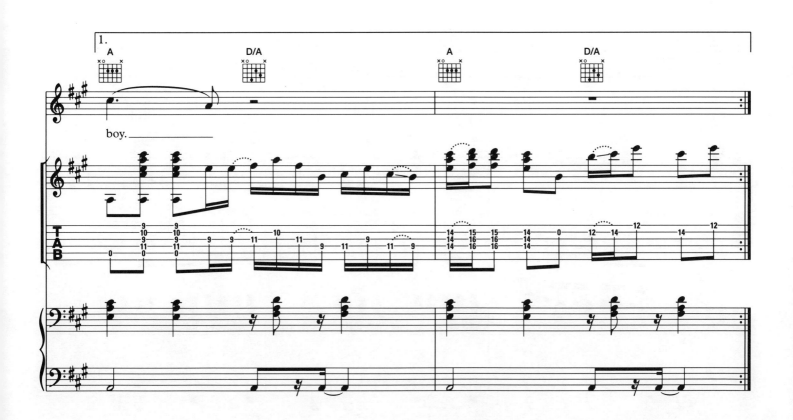

boy.__

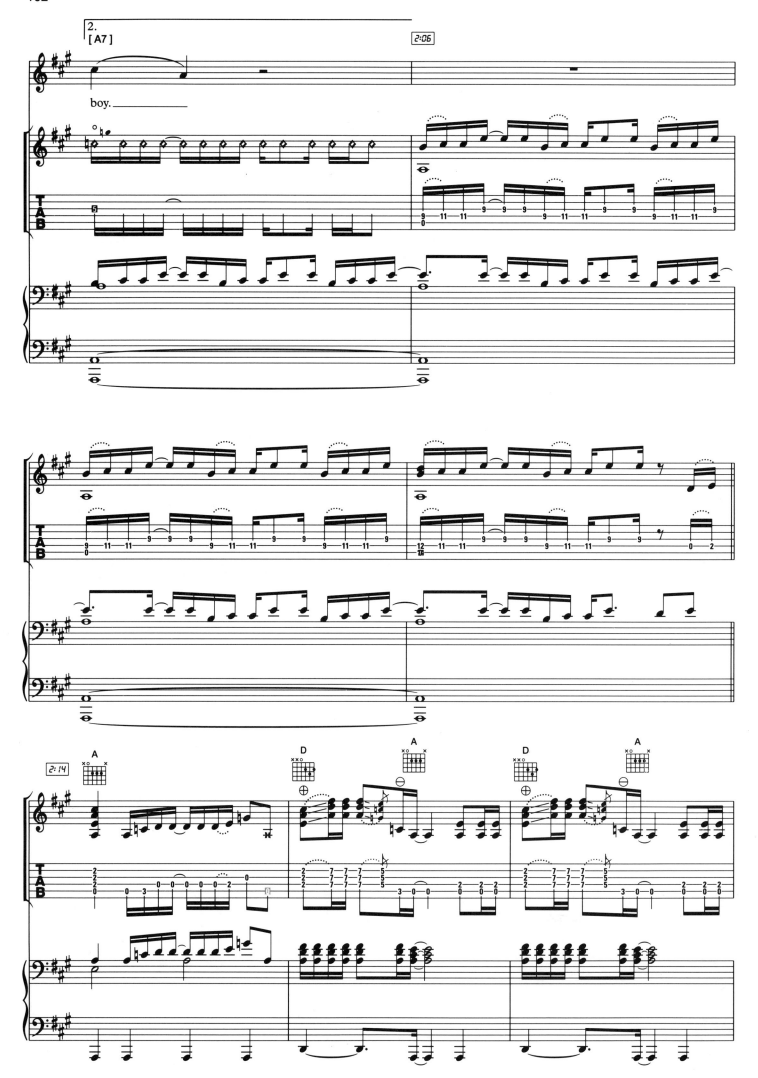

D.𝄋 al Coda

⊕ CODA

3. What do you

boy._____

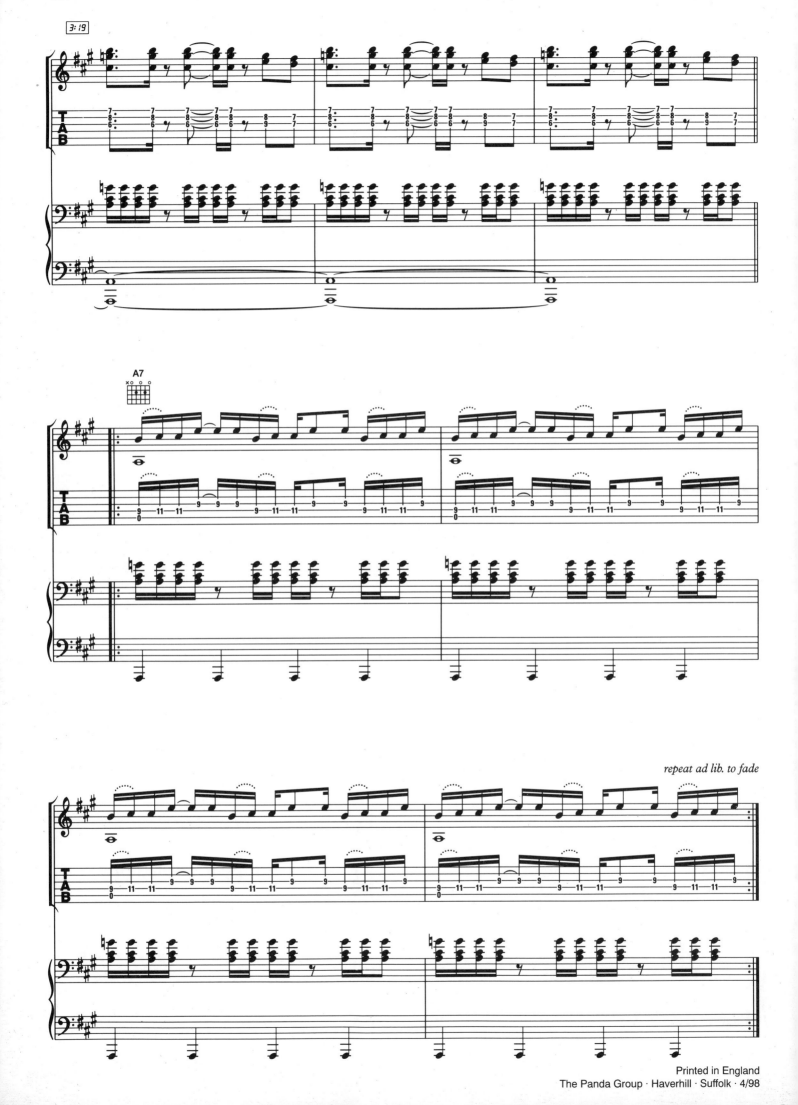

repeat ad lib. to fade

Printed in England
The Panda Group · Haverhill · Suffolk · 4/98